Steadwell Books World Tour

GERMANY

Christopher Mitten

Steadwell Books

Raintree Steck-Vaughn Publishers
A Harcourt Company

Austin · New York
www.raintreesteckvaughn.com

Published by Raintree Steck-Vaughn Publishers,
an imprint of Steck-Vaughn Company

Editor: Simone T. Ribke
Designer: Maria E. Torres

Library of Congress Cataloging-in-Publication Data
Mitten, Christopher.
    Germany / by Christopher Mitten.
        p. cm. -- (Steadwell books world tour)
    Includes bibliographical references and index.
    ISBN 0-7398-5754-1
    1. Germany--Juvenile literature. 2. Germany--Description and travel--Juvenile
literature. I. Title. II. Series.

    DD17 .M58 2002
    943--dc21   2002017868

Printed in the United States of America
1 2 3 4 5 6 7 8 9 10 WZ 07 06 05 04 03 02

Photo acknowledgments
Cover (a) ©H. Armstrong Roberts; cover (b) ©AFP/CORBIS; cover (c) ©Steve Vidler/eStock;
cover (d) ©Peter Harholdt/CORBIS; p.1a ©Bob Krist/CORBIS; p.1b ©Steve Vidler/eStock;
p.3a ©Steve Vidler/eStock; p.3b ©Bob Krist/CORBIS; p.5 ©H. Armstrong Roberts; p.6
©Kevin Galvin; p.7 ©Elsen/Mauritius/H. Armstrong Roberts; p.8 ©Alan Kaye/ DRK; p.13
©Bob Krist/CORBIS; p.14 ©Franz-Marc Frei/CORBIS; p.15 ©Kevin Galvin; p.16 ©Viesti
Associates, Inc.; p.19 ©Reuters NewMedia Inc./CORBIS; p.21a ©Photo Library International,
Ltd./eStock; p.21b ©Pictor/Uniphoto; p.25a ©Reuters NewMedia, Inc/CORBIS; p.25b Kevin
Galvin; p.26 ©Peter Harnholdt/CORBIS; p.27 ©Christopher Cormack/CORBIS; p.28 ©Owen
Franken/CORBIS; p.29 ©AFP/CORBIS; p.31a ©Dr. Lorenz/H. Armstrong Roberts; p.31b
©Kevin Galvin; p.33 ©Dallas and John Heaton/ CORBIS; p.34 © Dennis Gottlieb/FoodPix;
p.35 ©Bill Boch/FoodPix; p.37a ©Bob Krist/CORBIS; p.37b ©Tom Nebbia/CORBIS;
p.39a ©Kevin Galvin; p.39b ©Pat Armstrong/Visuals Unlimited; p.40 ©AFP/CORBIS;
p.41 Owen Franken/ CORBIS; p.42 ©Viesti Associates, Inc.; p.43b ©Bob Krist/CORBIS;
p.43c ©Richard T. Nowitz/CORBIS; p.44a,b ©Hulton Archive; p.44c ©Mitchell Gerber/
CORBIS.

Additional photography by Getty Images Royalty Free and Steck-Vaughn Collection.

CONTENTS

Welcome to Germany

Are you interested in Germany? If you are, the best way to learn about the country is to go there. In Germany you can explore **enchanted** forests and ancient castles. You can visit quiet villages and modern cities. Whether you are planning a visit, or just want to learn more, turn the page. Germany awaits!

A Tip to Get You Started

• *Use the Table of Contents*

Already know what you are looking for? Maybe you just want to know what topics this book will cover. The Contents page tells you what topics you will read about. It tells you where to find them in the book.

• *Look at the Pictures*

This book has lots of great photos. Flip through and check out those pictures you like the best. They will show you what the book is all about. Read the captions to learn even more about the photos.

• *Use the Glossary*

As you read this book, you may notice that some words appear in **bold** print. Look up bold words in the Glossary in the back of the book. The Glossary will help you learn what they mean.

▲ **PLEASURE DRIVE**
This world-famous German highway, the Autobahn, is 6,800 miles (11,000 km) long—perfect for sightseeing by car. There is no speed limit on the Autobahn.

Start your tour with Germany's past. To understand Germany today, it helps to know the history of what made this country so great.

Ancient History

German ancestors began to settle in the area about 5,500 years ago. Around 100 B.C., several German tribes came into contact with the Romans. In A.D. 9, the Romans attacked them but were defeated in the famous Battle of the Teutoburg Forest.

Age of Kings

Over the years, many different kings ruled Germany. Around A.D. 400, Germany was linked to France by a king named Clovis. Clovis came from a tribe called the Franks. He was important because he became a Christian. This helped spread the religion in Germany.

In A.D. 687, a family named the Carolingians came to power. Charlemagne was its most famous king. He expanded the kingdom. In 843, his kingdom was divided up among his grandsons. For the next 1,000 years, Germany remained divided into small kingdoms.

◀ **BOO!**
Gargoyles were used long ago to ward off evil spirits. In Germany, you will find gargoyles on many buildings. Pretty scary!

In 1517, one of the important events for all of Europe began in Germany: the Reformation. During the Reformation, the Protestant form of Christianity was **founded** by Martin Luther. In 1517, he nailed a piece of paper to the door of the main church in Wittenberg. It contained 95 ideas he had about Christianity. His ideas mostly criticized the Roman Catholic Church. Luther's ideas are now called "The 95 Theses." For 100 years after Luther's death, Catholics and Protestants fought all over Germany. Finally, in 1643, they declared a **truce** called the Peace of Westphalia.

Formation of a Nation

After the Reformation, most of the land that is now Germany was called Prussia. In 1860 Prussia was **unified** as Germany by a man named Otto Von Bismarck. He was **chancellor** under King Wilhelm I. In 1871, King Wilhelm I was renamed kaiser, or emperor, of Germany. Bismarck became known as the Iron Chancellor.

▲ **THE HOLOCAUST REMEMBERED**
This is the site of a German death camp at Dachau. The sign
is pointing to the shelters (bunkers) and the crematoriums
(krematorium). Millions of Jews died in German death camps
during the Holocaust.

World Wars and the Holocaust

The power of the new Germany grew over the next
40 years, alarming the other European countries. In 1914,
World War I began. Germany was defeated in 1918.

By 1929, Germany was in trouble because of a
worldwide **economic depression**. In 1934, the
National Socialist Party—the "Nazi" party—took over.

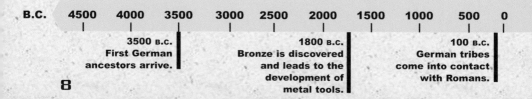

B.C.	4500	4000	3500	3000	2500	2000	1500	1000	500	0

3500 B.C.
First German
ancestors arrive.

1800 B.C.
Bronze is discovered
and leads to the
development of
metal tools.

100 B.C.
German tribes
come into contact
with Romans.

Adolf Hitler was the Nazi leader. He blamed Germany's problems on other European countries and on Jews. In 1939, Britain, France, and Russia declared war on Germany after Hitler invaded Poland. For the next six years, the entire world was at war.

During World War II, the Nazis committed a horrible crime. They rounded up Jewish people and sent them to **death camps**. More than six million Jewish men, women, and children were murdered in these camps. This terrible period in history is called the **Holocaust**.

Germany Divided, Germany Reunified

After the war, Germany was divided in two. Germany's capital, Berlin, was also divided. East Germany and East Berlin were **communist**. In 1961, the communists built a wall down the center of the city called the Berlin Wall.

Germany remained divided for 40 years. This period is often considered part of the **cold war**. The cold war came to an end when the Soviet Union ended. Then the Berlin Wall was torn down. In 1990, East and West Germany were finally reunited.

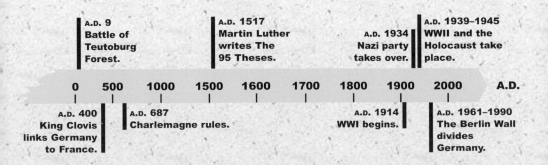

A.D. 9
Battle of Teutoburg Forest.

A.D. 1517
Martin Luther writes The 95 Theses.

A.D. 1934
Nazi party takes over.

A.D. 1939–1945
WWII and the Holocaust take place.

0   500   1000   1500   1600   1700   1800   1900   2000   A.D.

A.D. 400
King Clovis links Germany to France.

A.D. 687
Charlemagne rules.

A.D. 1914
WWI begins.

A.D. 1961–1990
The Berlin Wall divides Germany.

A LOOK AT GERMANY'S GEOGRAPHY

Do you wonder what Germany looks like? Picture a country with beautiful valleys, snowcapped mountains, and rushing rivers. If all that sounds good, Germany might just be the perfect place for you to visit. Want to learn more? Read on!

The Land

Germany lies in Central Europe. In the south are Germany's highest mountains, the Bavarian Alps. The highest peak in the Bavarian Alps and in Germany is called Zugspitze. It stands 9,718 feet (2,964 m) tall.

The Jura Mountains are also in the south. They are not as high as the Bavarian Alps. Their highest peaks are around 4,000 feet (1,200 m). The Jura Mountains overlap with Germany's Black Forest, or Schwarzwald. The Schwarzwald got its name from the dark evergreen trees that fill the forest.

To the north of the Bavarian Alps and the Black Forest lie the central uplands. The Harz Mountains are located here. The highest point in this region is Brocken Peak, which stands at 3,747 feet (1,136 m).

The northern region of Germany is a wet, low-lying plain. There are many rivers in this part of Germany and the surrounding soil is **fertile** and excellent for farming.

GERMANY'S SIZE ▶
Germany covers about 137,000 square miles (356,000 sq km). To Germany's north is Denmark. To the west lie the Netherlands, Belgium, Luxembourg, and France. To the south of Germany are Switzerland and Austria. To Germany's east are the Czech Republic and Poland.

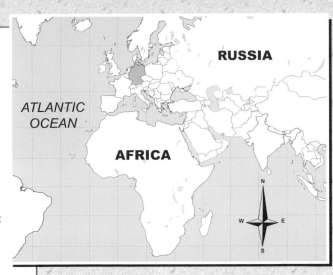

Water

Germany borders two seas. They are separated by the Jutland Peninsula. To the northwest of the Jutland Peninsula is the North Sea. To the northeast is the Baltic Sea. Germany contains several lakes; the biggest is Bodensee—Lake Constance in English.

Germany has several major rivers. The Danube River runs through the southern part of Germany. The Elbe River runs from the central uplands through the city of Hamburg, and into the North Sea. In the west lies the Rhine River. Each of these rivers flows through other countries. The Rhine provides a natural border between Germany and France.

GERMANY

★   National Capital

—   Rivers

▲ THE RHINE RIVER
People have lived along the Rhine River for centuries.
Above, an ancient castle overlooks the river.

The Weather

Germany has a **temperate** climate. The weather varies from region to region. In Hamburg, near the north coast, the high temperatures average about 52 degrees Fahrenheit (11°C) in the dead of winter. They average about 73 degrees (23°C) at the height of summer. High temperatures in Munich, in the far south of Germany, average about 33 degrees Fahrenheit (1°C) in the winter and 72 degrees (22°C) in the summer. The Bavarian Alps are the coldest and wettest area of Germany.

Overall, the average temperature in Germany during January is around 30 degrees Fahrenheit (0°C). During July, the average temperature rises to about 64 degrees (18°C).

▲ RAINY DAYS
Fall and winter bring chilly rain to Germany. It's a good idea to pack a coat and an umbrella if you visit during these seasons.

BERLIN: A BIG-CITY SNAPSHOT

▲ OVERLOOKING BERLIN
The city of Berlin has a lot to offer. It is both beautiful and busy.

No trip to Germany is complete without a trip to Berlin. Its wide boulevards, ancient buildings, and beautiful parks make this the perfect place to spend a week or two.

Berlin's Past

After World War II, Germany was divided in two parts—East and West Germany. The eastern half had a communist government like the Soviet Union (Russia and nearby countries). Berlin was also divided. In 1961, the Soviet Union built a wall through the middle of Berlin so people could not leave East Berlin for the West. In 1989, the people of Berlin tore down the wall.

West Berlin

The best place to start your tour of Berlin is the Tiergarten. It is a huge park. Tiergarten means "animal garden" in English. There is a beautiful zoo in the Tiergarten.

At the east end of the Tiergarten, you will find the Reichstag. It is home to the German parliament.

Head to the Kurfürstendamm to buy gifts for your friends. It is one of Berlin's shopping districts. Or visit the Berlin Museum. It tells the story of Berlin.

East Berlin

The best way to get to East Berlin is through Checkpoint Charlie. It is the most famous passageway between East and West Berlin. Nothing remains of the border crossing today. But there is an excellent museum there called Haus am Checkpoint Charlie. It tells how and why the Berlin Wall was constructed. It also tells the sad story of the hundreds of people who died while trying to escape East Berlin.

After leaving the museum, explore the area where the wall once stood. The wall is gone, but its remains are still there. Tourists used to chip little pieces off the wall as souvenirs. Today, the rubble that remains is protected. So do not try to take a piece home with you.

Next, walk to the Brandenburg Gate. This is one of the most impressive monuments in all of Berlin. It was built to celebrate German power.

South of the Berlin Wall, you will find the remains of Hitler's bunker. It was here that he committed suicide when he realized that he had lost the war. Hitler's bunker is now a **memorial** to the destruction and murder he caused during World War II and the Holocaust.

Continue east and you will come to Alexanderplatz, one of the most famous squares in Berlin. It was here that East Germans began to protest the Berlin Wall in 1989. A few days after the demonstrations, the wall was torn down. Alexanderplatz is not Berlin's most beautiful spot, but it is one of the most important. It is where Berlin began its new future.

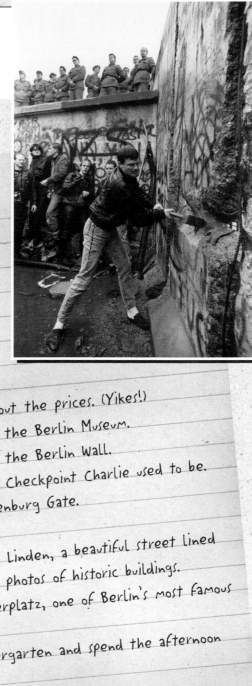

BERLIN WALL ▶
A demonstrator helps knock down the Berlin Wall. Until 1989, it separated East and West Berlin.

BERLIN'S TOP-10 CHECKLIST

If you are heading to Germany, here is a list of the top-10 things you have to do.

- ☐ Visit the Reichstag. See if you can spot a member of the parliament.
- ☐ Go shopping on the Kurfürstendamm. Check out the prices. (Yikes!)
- ☐ Spend the afternoon at the Berlin Museum.
- ☐ Head to the remains of the Berlin Wall.
- ☐ Pass to the East where Checkpoint Charlie used to be.
- ☐ Walk under the Brandenburg Gate.
- ☐ Visit Hitler's Bunker.
- ☐ Stroll down Unter den Linden, a beautiful street lined with trees. Snap some photos of historic buildings.
- ☐ Walk around Alexanderplatz, one of Berlin's most famous squares.
- ☐ Head back to the Tiergarten and spend the afternoon at its zoo.

Germany is a great country with lots of exciting places to visit. With so much to choose from, it may be hard to know where to start! Here are four suggestions that should probably be somewhere on your schedule.

Hamburg's Harbor

Hamburg was built on the mouth of the River Elbe, where it opens into the North Sea. Hamburg was founded by Charlemagne in A.D. 810 (see the chapter on Germany's history). Today, Hamburg is one of Europe's largest ports. About 15,000 ships come in and out of Hamburg each year. They carry everything from washing machines to lemons, and make Hamburg a center of international trade.

For travelers, this activity makes for great sightseeing. At times, a stroll along the harbor can get pretty gritty. The water, with all those ships and local industry along the river, can make for some unpleasant smells.

The best way to see Hamburg's harbor is to take a boat tour. The captain will take you right up next to the biggest ships in the world. You can watch as crates of coffee are carried into Germany while truck tires sail off to the Pacific Ocean.

You should also wander around the **docks** on foot. While you are there, make sure to check out the fish market. This is a great place to pick up a few live eels, three dozen oysters, or whatever else you think you will need on the rest of your trip.

▼ PORT SIDE
All kinds of worldly goods travel in and out of Hamburg's busy port.

FIX THIS! ▶
The harbor is also a place to see huge ships docked for repairs. Can you imagine trying to fix something so big?

▲ FAIRY-TALE CASTLE
This castle doesn't have a moat, a fire-breathing dragon, or a fairy-tale princess. It was built by King Ludwig II of Germany in the late 1800s.

Neuschwanstein

If you have ever seen Sleeping Beauty's castle at Disneyland then you know what Neuschwanstein (say, noy-SHVAN-shteen) castle looks like. Disney actually based its castles on this incredible building.

The castle was built by the local ruler, King Ludwig II, at the end of the 19th century. It is located near Munich, in the Bavarian Alps. The architecture was already old-fashioned, but the king wanted to live in a fairy-tale palace. In fact, the castle was designed by theater people who built sets for operas.

Sadly, Ludwig died soon after the castle was finished, so he never really got to live in his dream home. Still, he left behind a truly unique place for travelers to visit. Try to come in the evening. The sunsets from Ludwig's home are breathtaking.

FASCINATING FACT

When King Ludwig II built this castle in the 1800s, he made it very modern. All the toilets had automatic flushing. There was a hot water system for the kitchens and baths. There was even a warm-air heating system.

Oktoberfest

Oktoberfest is probably Germany's most famous festival. It is 16 days of eating, drinking, singing, and dancing. It takes place each fall in the city of Munich in southeast Germany. It starts on a Saturday in September and ends on the first Sunday in October. Millions of tourists come from all over the world to Oktoberfest. Why? It is a wild and fun celebration of German culture.

Oktoberfest started in 1810, when the people of Munich celebrated a royal wedding. The event included horse races. It was repeated the next year, and then the year after that, and so on. They no longer hold horse races, but the tradition of Oktoberfest lives on today.

Germans are world-famous **brewers** of beer. Oktoberfest is probably best known as a celebration of Germany's fine brews. Beer halls in Munich burst with visitors who crowd around long tables during this festival. People often sing German folk songs. They link arms and sway in time to the music as they sing. Sometimes they even get up and dance.

The festivities kick off with a parade. There are bands and music. There are horses, and people dressed in traditional German clothes. You might enjoy carnival rides, like roller coasters and Ferris wheels. You can sample traditional German cooking. Musical bands come from all over the world to play at this festival. If you like to party, then you are going to love Oktoberfest!

▲ PARADING ABOUT TOWN
This guy looks really happy to kick up his heels in an Oktoberfest parade!

JOIN THE BAND ▶
Young and old alike can enjoy the live music at Oktoberfest.

The Porsche Factory and Museum

If there is one thing Germany is famous for, it is fine automobiles. BMW, Mercedes, and Volkswagen are a few of the brands you might recognize. One of Germany's coolest (and most expensive) cars is the Porsche. This sleek sports car has long been the car of choice for movie stars and royalty. Can't come up with the cash for one just yet? You can still go to the Porsche factory and museum. It is located in the town of Stuttgart.

Start by taking a free guided tour through the factory. Watch the highly skilled workers carefully assemble each of the cars. You will see why Germans are known around the world for their top-quality cars.

Then head to the museum. There you can see Porsches from the past 50 years. They won't let you drive one, but they will let you take pictures next to the cars. These hot rods are beauties.

IN THE FAST LANE ▼
Germany is a great place to drive a fast car like a Porsche. There is no speed limit on the German superhighway, the Autobahn.

▼ NOT YOUR AVERAGE CAR FACTORY
Highly skilled workers take their time creating these dream-mobiles. Each one has to be perfect.

GOING TO SCHOOL IN GERMANY

Kids in Germany have to go to school for 12 years. After that, they are free to continue with school or leave to get a job. Usually Germans spend a year in kindergarten and about four years in elementary school.

After that, students go to one of four kinds of schools. The first is called a gymnasium, where students study general subjects such as math, language, and science. The second is called a hauptschule or a realschule. This is a **vocational school** that trains students for different kinds of jobs. At the third type of school, students study general subjects and also get job training. The fourth offers all three courses of study: the general subjects, the gymnasium course, and the hauptschule course.

Students are taught in German, the official language of Germany. German public schools are considered among of the best in the world.

◀ IN A GERMAN CLASSROOM
Students can pick from a variety of subjects in German schools. They may even choose to train for a certain job.

GERMAN SPORTS

In 1816, the bicycle was invented in Germany. Ever since, bicycling has been one of Germany's most popular sports. Germany hosts many international bike races, and Germans do very well in races in other countries.

Tennis is also popular in Germany. Two of the world's best tennis players, Boris Becker and Steffi Graf, are German. Today, many young people have followed their example and taken up tennis.

The most popular sport in Germany is soccer. Germany has a large national soccer league. What city has the best team? It depends on which fans you ask!

OLYMPIC GOLD ▶
Jens Lehmann rode his way to an Olympic gold medal in the 2000 Summer Games in Sydney, Australia. This was a big win for the country that invented bicycles!

FROM FARMING TO FACTORIES

Not all Germans make cars for a living—but many do. Germany is the third-largest car maker in the world, behind the United States and Japan. The German car industry brings many Deutsche marks—German money. Mercedes, Volkswagen, and Porsche are a few of these companies. They employ people to design the cars, build them, and then sell them all over the planet.

Germans manufacture numerous other products. These include plastics, electronics, textiles, and chemicals. The high quality of German products is recognized around the world. One reason German products are so good is because Germany has a great education system. Before a German person goes to work in a factory, he or she has probably learned many parts of the job in school. Generally, German factories produce goods that are difficult to make. They require a **skilled workforce**.

Some Germans are farmers. They grow grains like oats, wheat, and rye. Others grow vegetables, fruits, and sugar beets for sugar. Many raise animals, such as sheep, pigs, and cows. Germans use these goods to make food products like bread, sausage, and beer.

Other Germans work as doctors, lawyers, bus drivers, and barbers—all the sorts of jobs that keep any society going.

▲ **BREWING BEER**
Germans are known for enjoying many kinds of beer. Making the perfect brew is an art that takes patience and skill.

▲ **SHEARING SHEEP**
German farmers shear their sheep for wool. This wool is used around the world to make sweaters and other warm clothing.

THE GERMAN GOVERNMENT

The kind of government Germany has today is not very old—it started when East and West Germany were reunified in 1990. Germany is now a **democracy**. To become a leader here, you have to win an election.

Germany has two branches of federal government: the parliament, which makes the laws, and the executive, which carries them out. The parliament is divided into two parts: the Bundestag and the Bundesrat. The Bundestag is the more powerful section. It makes the laws for the whole country. The Bundesrat represents the different regions of Germany. Its members make laws that affect their home states—like education or health care.

The chancellor is head of the executive branch of government. The chancellor is chosen by the Bundestag and is the most powerful person in the German government.

GERMANY'S NATIONAL FLAG

The German flag has three bands of color. The top band is black, the middle is red, and the bottom is gold. This flag represents the reunification of East and West Germany.

RELIGIONS OF GERMANY

About 72% of Germans are Christians. They follow the teachings of a man named Jesus, as written in the New Testament of the Bible. About half of Germany's Christians are Roman Catholic. Catholics are Christians who also follow the teachings of the Pope, a religious leader who lives near Rome. The other half of German Christians are Protestant, which means that they do not follow the Pope's teachings.

Some 2% of Germans are Muslim. Muslims follow the teachings of Mohammed, written in a holy book called the Koran.

About 70,000 Jews live in Germany. They follow the teachings found in the Torah, or Old Testament of the Bible.

▲ HISTORIC CHURCHES
These magnificent buildings show the same love of detail as some of Germany's amazing castles.

GERMAN FOOD

After a long hike through the Black Forest, or a day of sailing on the North Sea, there is nothing better than sitting down to a meal at a German table. German food is hearty and comforting. It's perfect after an active day.

A typical main dish at a German lunch or dinner will be pork, beef, veal, or chicken. The meat is served with an elaborate sauce. Side dishes usually include potatoes, bread, and a vegetable—like carrots, beets, or cabbage.

Lighter meals may feature cheeses and preserved meats, sausage, ham, and pickled fish. At these meals, Germans eat lots of bread. If you visit Germany, be sure to try as many different kinds of bread as possible. Every one of them is delicious!

Breakfast in Germany is often coffee and pastries. Sometimes it includes cheese and cold sausage. If you are in the north, you might even get a piece of fish with your coffee.

◀ HOPE YOU'RE HUNGRY!
This hearty plate of food is a traditional German delight. Knockwurst is a type of sausage.

Germany's Recipe

KARTOFFELPUFFER (POTATO PANCAKES)

Ingredients:

9 medium raw potatoes

1 medium onion, chopped

3 eggs

1 tsp of salt

Pinch of pepper

6 tbsp flour

2 tbsp parsley

3 tbsp vegetable oil

WARNING:
Never cook or bake by yourself. Always have an adult assist you in the kitchen.

Directions:
Peel and grate potatoes. Drain liquid from potatoes. Mix potatoes, onion, eggs, salt, pepper, flour, and parsley. Heat oil in pan on medium. Put mixture in pan 3 tablespoons at a time. Flatten pancakes as they cook. Cook until they are golden brown on both sides.

UP CLOSE: THE BLACK FOREST

Mirror, mirror, on the wall, which is the most enchanted forest of all? Most people know about Germany through folk tales. Do you remember the stories of Hansel and Gretel, Sleeping Beauty, and Snow White? These stories all take place in German forests. To see fairy-tale forests up close, head to the Black Forest in southwest Germany.

The Southern Black Forest

The southern Black Forest is the most **remote** part. It borders on Switzerland and France. It is home to the highest mountains in the area.

A good place to start your journey is the Feldberg, the tallest mountain. It stands 4,899 feet (1,485 m) tall. You can see much of the Black Forest from its top.

When you have made it down the mountain, head to Lake Schluchsee. It is a huge lake fed by ancient **glaciers**. This is a great place to take a swim.

Next, visit the nearby abbey, or Christian religious settlement, called Kloster Saint Trudpert. The abbey is about 1,200 years old. It was built by Irish monks who wanted to spread Christianity to the area. Today it serves as a home for nuns. Monks and nuns are men and women who live away from society and serve God.

▼ WHEN THE FOG ROLLS IN

The Black Forest appears even more magical under the cover of fog. Tall, dark evergreens and high peaks poke out from this fog and greet the morning sky.

BIKING IN THE BLACK FOREST ▶

This is just one of many exciting things you can do in the Black Forest region.

The Central Black Forest

The city of Freiburg is often called the capital of the Black Forest. The first place to check out in Freiburg is the Münster. This church is one of the most beautiful in Germany. Locals started building the Münster in the year 1200. It is made from red stone. Don't miss the colorful stained glass windows inside. They are almost 700 years old!

Next, go west to Freiburg's university. The buildings of the old university are definitely worth a tour. Getting hungry? Head to one of the local restaurants for a hearty German lunch. Try German sausages, cabbage, and (of course) Black Forest cake with chocolate and cherries.

The Northern Black Forest

The northern region of the Black Forest is a great place to take some photos. It is filled with dark, hidden valleys, ancient bridges, and thick woodland. Hikers will find some of the best trails around the Nagold River and the Murg River.

One of the best ways to end a visit to the Black Forest is in Baden–Baden. This town has always been a top vacation spot for Europe's rich and famous. There are many health **spas** here. They are perfect for getting some rest and exercise before returning to the modern world. There are beautiful gardens to explore. You can even take golf lessons at the famous golf course.

◀ IN FREIBURG
Walking around Freiburg is the best way to experience its charm. These buildings look like life-size gingerbread houses.

LICHEN ▶
Lichen (say: LEE-shin) are tiny plants that grow on the sides of rocks and trees. You can see many different colors and varieties of lichen in the Black Forest.

HOLIDAYS

Germans celebrate more holidays than most other countries in Europe. German Unity Day is October 3. It is a national holiday that celebrates Germany's **reunification** in 1990. Oktoberfest, in the fall, offers 16 days of parades, carnivals, music, and more.

Many of the major holidays in Germany are Christian holidays. Christmas, celebrating the birth of Jesus, is the most important of these. Easter is also important for Germans. Easter commemorates Jesus's rebirth.

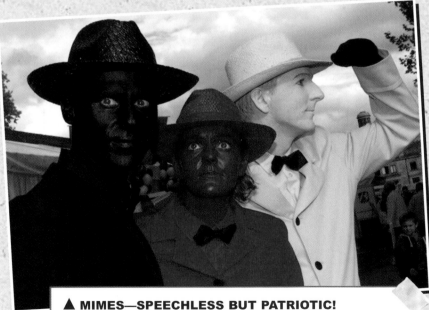

▲ MIMES—SPEECHLESS BUT PATRIOTIC!
Three mimes wear the German colors at a German Unity Day celebration.

LEARNING THE LANGUAGE

English	German	How to say it
Good day	Guten tag	GOO-ten TAHG
Good morning	Guten morgen	GOO-ten MOR-gun
Goodbye	Auf wiedersehen	OFF VEE-der-zay-en
Thank you	Danke schön	DAHN-keh SHOON
You're welcome	Bitte schön	BIH-teh SHOON
My name is _____	Ich heisse _____	EESH HI-seh____
I'm from _____	Ich komme aus	EESH KOM-meh OWS

QUICK FACTS

GERMANY

Capital ▶
Berlin

Borders
Denmark, Baltic Sea (N)
Poland, Czech Republic (E)
Australia, Switzerland (S)
France, Luxembourg,
Belgium, Netherlands (W)

Area
137,803 square miles
(221,766 sq km)

Population
30,339,770

▼ **Main Religious Groups**

Largest Cities
Berlin (3,477,900 people)
Hamburg (1,703,800)
Munich (1,251,100)
Cologne (963,300)
Frankfurt (656,200)

Roman Catholic (Christian) 34%

Protestant (Christian) 38%

— **Other religions or unaffiliated 26%**

— **Muslim 2%**

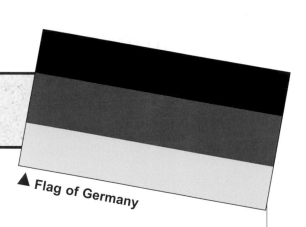

▲ Flag of Germany

Coastline
1,385 miles (2,220 km)

Longest River ▶
The Rhine
820 miles (1,320 km)

Literacy Rate
99% of people in Germany
can read and write

Major Industries
Food products, brewing,
textiles, clothing

▼ Monetary Units
Deutsche mark and euro

Chief Crops
Wheat, barley, rye, potatoes,
sugar beets, fruit, cattle,
pigs, poultry

Natural Resources
Iron production, steel, coal,
cement, chemicals, machinery,
vehicles, machine tools,
electronics, food and beverages,
metal fabrications, brown coal,
shipbuilding, machine building,
textiles, petroleum refining,
hides and skins

PEOPLE TO KNOW

◀ ANNE FRANK

Anne Frank was a German Jew born in 1929. When the Nazis came to power, she and her family went into hiding. Eventually, Anne was discovered and sent to a concentration camp where she died. While in hiding, Anne kept a diary. Today this diary has been read by millions all over the world. It is one of the most moving accounts of the Holocaust.

GERHARD SCHROEDER ▶

Gerhard Schroeder did not start out thinking he would be a famous politician. In fact, he wanted to be a salesman. After joining the Social Democratic Party, though, he became interested in politics. In 1998, he was named chancellor of Germany. Schroeder was born in 1944.

◀ STEFFI GRAF

Steffi Graf was born in 1969. She made it big in tennis when she was just a teenager, winning all four of the world's major tournaments in 1988. She went on to win each of them several more times. Over the years, this pro has won more than 20 million dollars in prize money!

MORE TO READ

Want to know more about Germany? Check out the books below.

The Anne Frank House. *Anne Frank in the World*. New York: Knopf, 2001.

Learn more about Anne Frank's touching story and about the Holocaust, with photos of the attic Anne and her family hid in during that time.

Dahl, Michael S. *Germany*. Mankato, MN: Capstone Press Inc., 1997.

Discover more about Germany through full-color photos.

Knorr, Rosanne and Knorr, John. *If I Lived in Germany*. Marietta, GA: Longstreet Press, 1992.

Explore what it would be like to live in Germany.

Spiegelman, Art. *Maus: A Survivor's Tale*. New York: Pantheon Books, 1992.

Examine the Holocaust up-close in this graphical book where the Jews are portrayed as mice and the Germans as cats.

Stein, Richard Conrad. *Berlin*. Danbury, CT: Children's Press, 1997.

Take a closer look around Berlin and see what it has to offer.

Wright, Nicola and Wooley, Kim. *Getting to Know Germany and German*. Hauppauge, NY: Barron's Educational Series, Inc., 1993.

Get to know Germany and German through this delightful book.

GLOSSARY

Brewers (BROO-urz)—people who make beer

Chancellor (CHAN-suh-lur)—the title of a leader of a country

Cold war (KOLD WORE)—conflict between the United States and the Soviet Union that stopped short of armed warfare

Communist (KOM-you-nist)—a government in which the state owns all the industry and assigns jobs to the people

Death camps (DETH KAMPS)—Nazi prison camps where Jews and other prisoners were taken to be killed

Democracy (di-MOCK-ruh-see)—a government with leaders who are elected by the people

Docks (DOKS)—landing areas where ships load and unload cargo or stay for repairs

Economic depression (ee-kuh-NOM-ik di-PRESH-un)—a time when businesses do badly and people cannot make any money

Enchanted (en-CHAN-tid)—something or someplace that seems magical

Fertile (FERT-il)—good for growing crops

Founded (FOWN-did)—to have started or set up something

Glaciers (GLAY-shurz)—large sheets of ice found near the North and South poles

Holocaust (HOLE-uh-kost)—the murder of six million Jews by the Nazis during World War II

Memorial (meh-MOR-ee-uhl)—a building or place that reminds people of an event from the past

Remote (rih-MOTE)—far away or hard to get to

Reunification (rih-YOU-ni-fi-KAY-shun)—two sides coming back together after being divided

Skilled workforce (SKILD WERK-fors)—the men and women who have the ability to do complicated jobs

Spas (SPAHZ)—resorts with baths that help heal and relax people

Temperate (TEM-per-it)—not too hot or too cold

Truce (TROOS)—an agreement to stop fighting

Unified (YOU-ni-fide)—brought together as one country or unit

Vocational school (voh-KAY-shuhn-uhl SKOOL)—school that teaches a trade or job

INDEX